D0116230

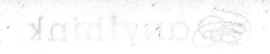

FUN FACT FILE: SPACE!

20 FUN FACTS ABOUT ROCKY PLANETS

By Heather Moore Niver

Gareth Stevens
PUBLISHING

Please visit our website, www.garethstevens.com. For a free color catalog of all our high-quality books, call toll free 1-800-542-2595 or fax 1-877-542-2596.

Library of Congress Cataloging-in-Publication Data

Niver, Heather Moore.
20 fun facts about rocky planets / by Heather Moore Niver.
p. cm. — (Fun fact file: space!)
Includes index.
ISBN 978-1-4824-1009-9 (pbk.)
ISBN 978-1-4824-1010-5 (6-pack)
ISBN 978-1-4824-1008-2 (library binding)
1. Inner planets — Juvenile literature. I. Niver, Heather Moore. II. Title.
QB606.N58 2015
523.4—d23

First Edition

Published in 2015 by
Gareth Stevens Publishing
111 East 14th Street, Suite 349
New York, NY 10003

Designer: Sarah Liddell
Editor: Greg Roza

Photo credits: Cover, p. 1 (Mars) Stocktrek Images/Getty Images; cover, p. 1 (stars) nienora/
Shutterstock.com; p. 5 fluidworkshop/Shutterstock.com; pp. 6–7 (stars) Procy/Shutterstock.com; pp. 6, 7, 24, 25
(planets) Tristan3D/Shutterstock.com; p. 8 Rob Wilson/Shutterstock.com; p. 9 Mopic/Shutterstock.com;
pp. 10, 11 photo courtesy of NASA/John Hopkins University Applied Physics Laboratory/Carnegie Institute of
Washington; p. 12 RHorning/Wikimedia Commons; p. 13 BlueRingMedia/Shutterstock.com; pp. 14, 20 photo
courtesy of NASA; p. 15 photo courtesy of NASA/JPL; p. 16 leonello calvetti/Shutterstock.com; p. 17 Johan
Swanepoel/Shutterstock.com; p. 18 photo courtesy of NASA/NOAA/GSFC/Suomi NPP/VIIRS/Norman Kuring;
p. 19 Vadim Sadovsky/Shutterstock.com; p. 21 photo courtesy of NASA/JPL-Caltech/MSSS; p. 22 JPL/Staff/
AFP/Getty Images; p. 23 NASA/Wikimedia Commons; pp. 24–25 (stars) Mihai-Bogdan Lazar/
Shutterstock.com; p. 26 photo courtesy of NASA Ames/JPL-Caltech; p. 27 photo courtesy of NASA/JPL-Caltech;
p. 29 Stocktrek Images/Stocktrek Images/Getty Images.

Printed in the United States of America

CPSIA compliance information: Batch #CS15GS: For further information contact Gareth Stevens, New York, New York at 1-800-542-2595.

Contents

Words in the glossary appear in **bold** type the first time they are used in the text.

Rock Out!

Our solar system is made up of the sun and all the smaller objects that **orbit** it. The largest objects are the eight planets. Of all the planets scientists have discovered, there are two basic kinds: rocky and **gaseous**.

You can probably guess how they got their names. Rocky planets are made out of rock and metal. Mercury, Venus, Earth, and Mars are all rocky planets. Gaseous planets are made mostly of gas. Jupiter, Saturn, Uranus, and Neptune are all gaseous planets.

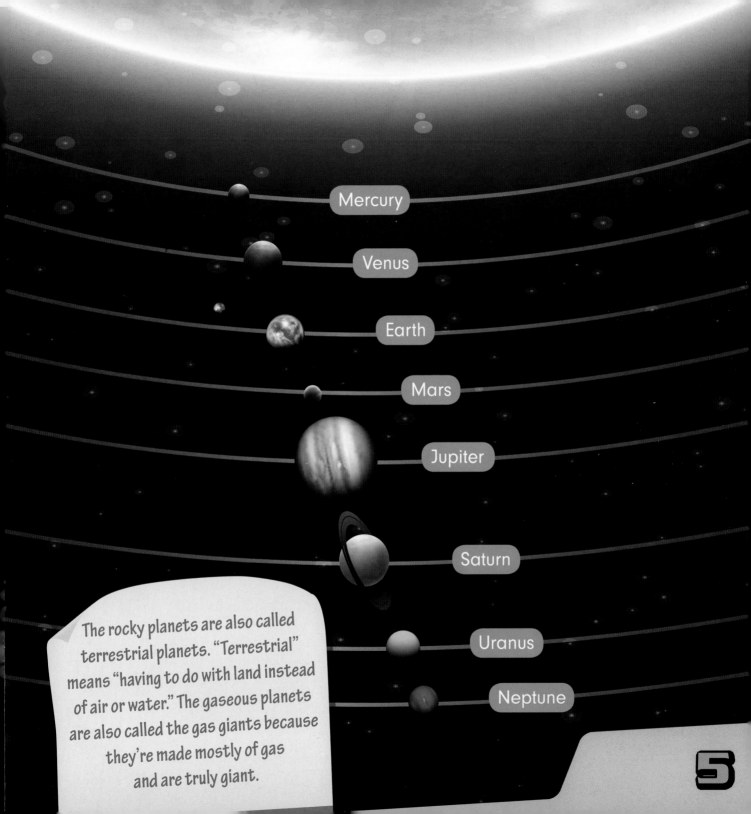

Mercury

Venus

Earth

Mars

Jupiter

Saturn

Uranus

Neptune

The rocky planets are also called terrestrial planets. "Terrestrial" means "having to do with land instead of air or water." The gaseous planets are also called the gas giants because they're made mostly of gas and are truly giant.

Solar Neighborhoods

The solar system is separated into two "neighborhoods" — inner and outer.

When the solar system first formed about 4.5 billion years ago, heavier matter stayed closer to the sun. Gases were blown away from the sun. This is why the inner planets are rocky and the outer planets are gaseous.

Mercury

Venus

Rocky planets wear less "jewelry" than the gas giants.

Compared to the gas planets, the rocky planets are small. The rocky planets don't have rings like Saturn and the other gas giants. Only Earth and Mars have moons, but the gas giants have more than 160 moons altogether.

Earth

Mars

Magnificent Mercury

FACT 3

Mercury races around the sun.

Mercury orbits the sun in just 88 days. This is the shortest amount of time of all the planets. The ancient Romans noticed how quickly Mercury moved and named it after the ancient Roman god with the same name.

Mercury was the swift-moving messenger of the gods. He's often shown with wings on his ankles.

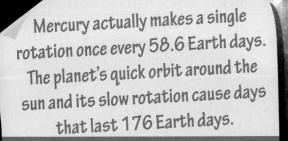

Mercury actually makes a single rotation once every 58.6 Earth days. The planet's quick orbit around the sun and its slow rotation cause days that last 176 Earth days.

Time as we know it is all messed up on Mercury.

Planets rotate, or spin around an **axis**. Standing on Mercury's surface, it takes 176 Earth days for the sun to rise, set, and then rise again. This means a "day" on Mercury is about twice as long as a "year" on Mercury!

You'd want to wear a lot of sunscreen on Mercury. And bring a sweater.

Mercury is the closest planet to the sun. That means it's one of the hottest planets. During the day, temperatures can get as high as 800°F (430°C)! At night, temperatures can drop to –292°F (–180°C). Brrrr!

Mercury doesn't have an atmosphere, which is a layer of gases around a planet. This means Mercury doesn't have weather. It also means there's nothing to hold the heat in at night.

Most of what we know about Mercury we learned in the early 1970s from the unmanned *Mariner 10* spacecraft. NASA's *Messenger* spacecraft took clearer images of the planet between 2008 and 2011.

FACT 6

Mercury has more in common with our moon than with Earth.

Mercury and Earth are very different. Mercury's surface is a lot like our moon's surface. Both have lots of rocks and craters. Scientists haven't found water or air on Mercury, but some water might be hiding beneath the surface, as on the moon.

FACT 7

Venus and Earth are almost twins.

Venus and Earth are almost the same size. Both planets are made up of the same rocky material. Venus has **volcanoes**, too. It even has a mountain range taller than the Himalayas! Of all the planets, Venus passes closest to Earth.

Venus

Earth

Venus and Earth are sometimes called sister planets.

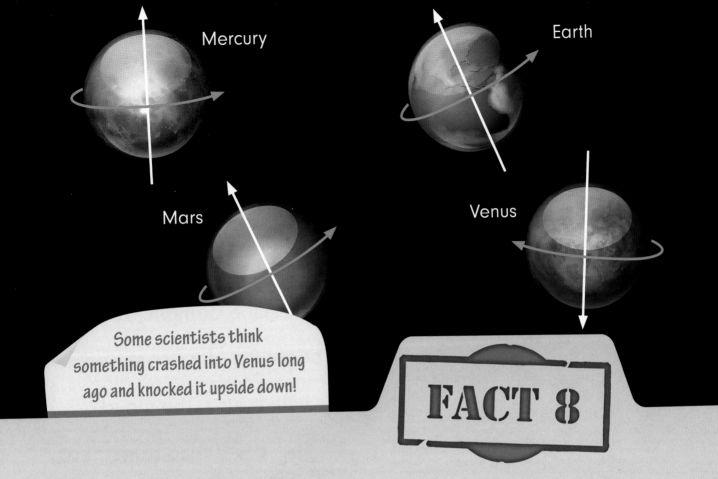

Mercury

Earth

Mars

Venus

Some scientists think something crashed into Venus long ago and knocked it upside down!

Venus spins backward.

All planets orbit the sun in a counterclockwise direction. Most of the planets rotate counterclockwise around their axis, too. Venus is the only rocky planet that rotates clockwise. This is called **retrograde** rotation. Uranus is the only other planet to do this.

Venus is the shiniest planet. It's also the hottest.

Venus is the second-closest planet to the sun. Thick clouds on Venus reflect sunlight, which makes it shine at night. Venus is so bright it's often confused with a star. The cloud cover also traps heat, making it the hottest planet— even hotter than Mercury!

The temperature on Venus can reach 869°F (465°C). That's hot enough to melt lead!

This image of Venus's surface was made using imaging radar. This area is called Alpha Regio.

FACT 10

Walking on Venus would feel like walking through water.

About 96 percent of Venus's atmosphere is made of the gas **carbon dioxide**. This is the gas our lungs get rid of when we breathe out. The carbon dioxide around Venus is so thick that walking on the planet's surface would feel like wading through water.

FACT 11

Earth has layers, somewhat like a cake.

Earth is the largest rocky planet by **diameter** and mass.

It has three layers. The crust is a very thin "icing" of rock and water. The mantle is hotter and softer, and currents of heat travel through it. The core is made mostly of very hot metals.

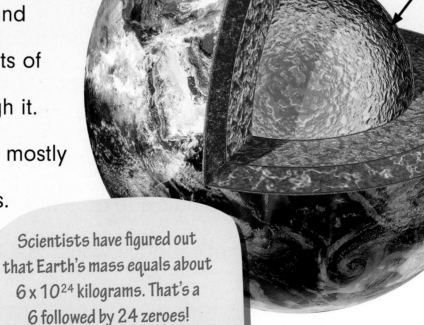

crust

mantle

core

Scientists have figured out that Earth's mass equals about 6×10^{24} kilograms. That's a 6 followed by 24 zeroes!

Scientists think Earth's outer core is mostly liquid iron. They think the inner core is mostly solid iron.

Earth's core is as hot as the surface of the sun.

Earth's core is a hot, **dense** place. It gets as hot as 10,832°F (6,000°C). That's the same temperature as the surface of the sun!

The core is rich with a metal called iron. It also contains nickel and tiny amounts of other metals.

There's no place like home!

So far, scientists haven't found any planets like Earth. No other planet has such large amounts of water on its surface and oxygen in its atmosphere. About 70 percent of Earth's surface is covered with water, so it looks blue from space.

Earth's atmosphere allows it to have weather. It also allows plants and animals to survive.

The Goldilocks zone is not too hot for life, and it's not too cold…it's just right!

FACT 14

We live in the "Goldilocks zone."

Earth is the only planet we know of that supports life.

Astronomers think this might be because Earth is located in the

"Goldilocks **zone**." This is a very small range near a star where

conditions are just right for life to exist.

FACT 15

Mars is rusty.

Mars is the fourth planet from the sun. Its reddish surface gives it the nickname the "Red Planet." That red-orange color comes from the rust in its rocks. Winds carry dust up into the atmosphere, which makes the air look pinkish red, too.

The iron in Mars's surface reacts with water and oxygen to form iron oxide, or rust.

In 2007, a break in a dust storm allowed an unmanned spacecraft to take this photograph of the Martian surface.

FACT 16

Some days, Mars plays hide-and-seek.

Mars has a lot of wild winds that can cause crazy dust storms. These storms change the planet's surface every day through **erosion**. Some storms are so powerful that the dust hides the entire planet from view!

Hellas Planitia is 4 times deeper than the Grand Canyon, perhaps deeper. Most of western Europe would fit inside it.

FACT 17

Mars has the biggest crater in the solar system.

The surface of Mars has a lot of craters. Most of them were probably created when space rocks hit the planet billions of years ago. Hellas Planitia is the largest crater in the solar system. It's more than 1,400 miles (2,253 km) across.

Mars has the biggest volcano in the solar system.

Mars has five giant volcanoes. The biggest one is called

Olympus Mons. It's the biggest

volcano in the solar system.

It's about the same size

as the state of Arizona.

Olympus Mons is far

taller than Mount

Everest, the tallest

mountain on Earth!

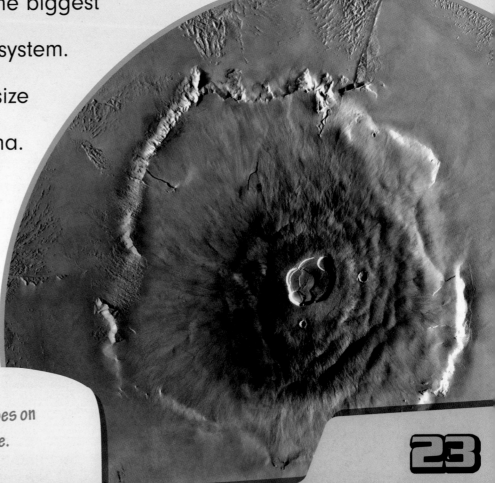

None of the volcanoes on
Mars are active.

Rockin' Facts

Want to compare and contrast the rocky planets? These charts will show you how they measure up.

MERCURY

diameter	3,030 miles (4,900 km)
length of day in Earth days	176
length of year in Earth years	0.24
average distance from the sun	36,000,000 miles (58,000,000 km)
average surface temperature	332°F (167°C)
number of moons	0

VENUS

diameter	7,500 miles (12,100 km)
length of day in Earth days	243
length of year in Earth years	0.67
average distance from the sun	67,200,000 miles (108,200,000 km)
average surface temperature	867°F (464°C)
number of moons	0

MARS

diameter	4,224 miles (6,800 km)
length of day in Earth days	1.03
length of year in Earth years	1.88
average distance from the sun	141,600,000 miles (228,000,000 km)
average surface temperature	−82°F (−63°C)
number of moons	2

EARTH

diameter	7,926 miles (12,760 km)
length of day in Earth days	1 (24 hours)
length of year in Earth years	1 (365 days)
average distance from the sun	93,000,000 miles (149,600,000 km)
average surface temperature	59°F (15°C)
number of moons	1

Out of This World!

FACT 19

Scientists have discovered alien rocky planets.

In January 2014, scientists reported that NASA's Kepler space telescope had discovered 16 new planets. They're called alien planets because they're outside of our solar system. Five of them are rocky planets.

The Kepler space telescope, launched in 2009, is a space observatory that searches for Earthlike planets in other solar systems.

Scientists will continue to search for alien rocky planets that are similar to Earth. Who knows, they may even find alien life!

Scientists may have discovered alien rocky planets, but most aren't in the Goldilocks zone.

Two of the new rocky planets are called Kepler-99b and Kepler-406b. They're both 40 percent larger than Earth. Scientists don't think they'll find life on them. It takes less than 5 days for these planets to orbit their stars, so it's too hot for life to survive on them.

27

Far-Out Rocks

The planets in our solar system will always be interesting to us. Scientists will send more unmanned spacecraft to visit inner planets, outer planets, and objects far beyond, too.

Small bodies of rock and ice orbit far, far away from the sun, outside the orbit of gas giant Neptune. Scientists call these objects trans-Neptunian objects (TNOs). They include the dwarf planets Pluto and Eris, and many other rocky bodies. Scientists hope to discover more about this rocky area in the years to come.

Scientists hope to send spacecraft to study Pluto and other TNOs in the near future.

Glossary

astronomer: a person who studies stars, planets, and other heavenly bodies

axis: an imaginary straight line around which a planet turns

carbon dioxide: a gas that animals breathe out and plants breathe in

dense: packed very closely together

diameter: the distance from one side of a round object to another through its center

erosion: a wearing down of the land by natural forces, such as wind and water

gaseous: made up of gases

orbit: to travel in a circle or oval around something, or the path used to make that trip

retrograde: backward or opposite the normal direction

volcano: an opening in a planet's surface through which hot, liquid rock sometimes flows

zone: an area that stands apart from other nearby areas

For More Information

Books

Coupe, Robert. *Earth's Place in Space*. New York, NY: PowerKids Press, 2014.

Lee, Pascal. *Mission: Mars*. New York, NY: Scholastic Books, 2013.

Miller, Ron. *Seven Wonders of the Rocky Planets and Their Moons*. Minneapolis, MN: Twenty-First Century Books, 2011.

Websites

Astronomy for Kids

kidsastronomy.com
Learn about rocky planets and other awesome things in space with games and more!

ESA Kids

www.esa.int/esaKIDSen/index.html
Check out this website from the European Space Agency to learn about all the planets and other cool things in outer space.

NASA Kids' Club

www.nasa.gov/audience/forkids/kidsclub/flash/
Kids of all ages will learn about the planets and space. See astronauts in space, too!

Index